Usher Parsons

Indian Names of Places in Rhode Island

Usher Parsons

Indian Names of Places in Rhode Island

ISBN/EAN: 9783743321724

Manufactured in Europe, USA, Canada, Australia, Japa

Cover: Foto ©ninafisch / pixelio.de

Manufactured and distributed by brebook publishing software
(www.brebook.com)

Usher Parsons

Indian Names of Places in Rhode Island

INDIAN NAMES

OF

PLACES IN RHODE-ISLAND:

COLLECTED BY

USHER PARSONS, M. D.,

FOR THE R. I. HISTORICAL SOCIETY.

———————

PROVIDENCE:
KNOWLES, ANTHONY & CO., PRINTERS.
1861.

PREFACE.

The Narraganset nation or tribe by whom this vocabulary was used, were in early times the most numerous and powerful of all the eastern Indians. They inhabited nearly all the present State of Rhode Island, including the islands in the bay, Block Island and the east end of Long Island. Their dominion extended northward to the Nipmucks in Providence county, and by conquest, eastward from the Pawcatuck river to the Merrimack. They were the most civilized and commercial tribe in New England, and so numerous, that, at one time, they could bring five thousand warriors into the field, " and one could meet a dozen of their towns in the course of twenty miles travel."

The Narraganset language was considered a variety of the Delaware, and extended some hundreds of miles, but varied in its idioms within a comparatively short distance. It has ceased to be a spoken language in the tribe for nearly half a century. The best records of it remaining, are Roger Williams' key to the Indian language, and the Apostle Elliot's Bible and Grammar, and Cotton's Vocabulary.

In 1766, the Narragansets were reduced to three hundred and fifteen persons, residing on the Indian reserved lands, in Charlestown. In 1832, the number was precisely the same, but only seven of them were pure blooded. Last year, the number was reduced to two of three-fourths blood, ten of half blood, forty-two of quarter blood, and sixty-eight of less than quarter blood, the total being 122 who claim descent from the original Narraganset tribe, and all of them exhibiting marks of the race.

No attempt is herein made, by the author, to examine Indian names of places as a philologist or grammarian, but merely to gather such as were in existence when civilization commenced, within the State of Rhode Island, according to its present boundary, and to indicate, as near as practicable, their exact locality; and, in a few instances, give the meaning or derivation of the word used.

I was led to this enterprise partly for the amusement it might afford in leisure hours, but more for the purpose of rescuing from oblivion names of places in use among the aborigines, and for the convenience of those who may hereafter wish to apply them to their country villas, factories, or institutions, as has often been done in this and other states.

For a more particular and faithful recent history of this remnant of the Indian race in this State, the reader is referred to the elaborate general history of Rhode Island, by Hon. Samuel G. Arnold, a work that reflects great credit on his patient and extensive research, and entitles him to the reputation of a candid, faithful and liberal-minded historian.

REMARKS.

The syllable *et* in Indian words seems equivalent to *place* or location. It is often found at the end of Indian names of places as hunting, planting, fishing, &c. Thus, Seconnet is a compound of Seki, *black*, and konk, *goose*. By dropping the syllable *ki* in the radicle *seki*, annexing *konk* and adding *et*, we have Seconknet, and by dropping the *k*, for the sake of euphony, and adding the syllable *et*, we have the word *Seconnet*, equivalent to wild or black-goose *place* or haunt. It is believed that in early times geese, in their annual migrations, stopped here to feed. The same meaning is attached to Seckonk, which has the same radical but not the affix *et*, probably it had gone out of use, the original name being Seckonket. Something analogous to this may be seen in our use of the word ton or town, as in Waterton or town, and Stonington, implying Water-place and Stony-place, the last syllable, *ton*, being affixed like *et* in Indian. It is a curious coincidence, that in one hundred towns or places, taken promiscuously, there will be found about as many *tons* or *towns* as there are *ets* or *etts* in an equal number of Indian towns or places; and that in the several hundred words here collected it occurs more than forty times.*

Sometimes the terminal syllable of words is dropped, and

* The terminal syllable *et* is often, but improperly, spelled *ett*.

et is substituted. Thus, in Nemascus or Nemaskish, by dropping the *us* or *ish* and substituting *et*, we have *Nemasket*, that is fish-place, well known in Boston harbor. So of the word Pawtucket, the two first syllables mean water-fall at the head of tide water, the final *et* added makes *water-fall-place.*

Another frequent terminal syllable of Indian names, besides *et* is *aug, og, oc,* and *auke,* probably all meaning the same, and therefore used indifferently, and written, originally, as the sound happened to strike different ears. A literary friend whom I consulted, thought that from its frequently ending the names of fishes, the *aug,* &c. might have a generic signification, and that the preceding syllables denote the kind of fishes, and that, as we say in English, dog-fish, cod-fish and cat-fish, so the Indians might add aug to taut, and make tautaug, and that minnehchaug, scupaug and quahaug may be formed in like manner, and the conjecture seemed to derive strength from the fact that names of places ending in aug, og, &c. are so frequently applied to fishing places. A more probable explanation, however is, that the aug, oc, &c. are the plural added to the singular, since whatever the singular terminal syllable of words may be, the plural is formed, not by the addition of *s* as in English words, but by *aug, oc,* &c. For Indian nouns are divided, not into genders like English, but into *animate* and *inanimate.* The animate form is, when the thing signified is a living creature, and such nouns do always form their plural by adding to the singular aug, oc, &c. Thus, washketomp, *man* is rendered plural by adding aug, oc, &c., making wasketompaug or oc, *men ;* and so nunksquan, *a girl,* is made nunksquaug or og, *girls.* So the noun *ox,* which the Indians derived from the English, is rendered in their plural oxcog, *oxen.* Thus, making all nouns plural of animate objects to end in aug, oc, og, &c. must furnish an abundant supply of words of such terminal syllables, without referring to fish alone.*

* The plural of inanimate nouns ends in *ash* as hussun, a stone is hussunash in the plural; and mepit, a tooth, is mepitash, teeth, in the plural.

The classification of verbal sounds into labials, dentals, nasals and gutturals, shows, when applied to the language of civilized, as compared with barbarous nations, that the gutturals prevail most in the latter, and labials in the former; that as civilization and mental and vocal culture advance, the articulate sounds of language, formed first in the throat, advance forward toward the lips.

The mute labials as they are called, p and b, are mere explosive sounds and occur in all tongues; and in the Indian the p is quite frequent, but f and v, requiring the concurrent action of the lips and teeth (and hence called dento-labials,) are not found in Indian names. The four or five hundred names of places here collected, present no instance of f or v, whilst the guttural sounds are very numerous and strongly characteristic of Indian utterance, as in Annaquatucket, Conockonoquit, Connanicut, Neutaconquenut, and furthermore, the Chippewa version of the Lord's prayer contains neither f nor v, but is made up of guttural sounds, whilst in the English version labial words occur more than ten times, and a guttural sound not once. The letters t, d, s, z and soft g or j are called dentals. The two first, viz: t and d, are mute dentals, and like p and b abound in all languages; s and d are hissing dentals, as in *say* and *as*, and are of frequent occurrence, but lisping dentals, namely *the* and *eth*, as in *scythe* and *these*, rarely if ever occur in the Indian tongue.

Differences in the mode of spelling Indian names of places are very apparent in written documents and records, attributable to various dialects, but more to the changes in the language, as uttered at different periods of time; thus, R. Williams spelled Narraganset, Cocumscusset and Quonanicut three different ways, at distant periods.in his career.

INDIAN NAMES.

A.

Aquidy or **Aquiduic**. NEWPORT, or rather Rhode Island, sometimes written Aquethnick, the middle syllable guttural. The word means longest island. It was deeded to Coddington by Canonicus and Miantinomy.

Apponaug, VILLAGE, named from a small river, so called, running into the head of Greenwich Bay, at Coweset. The meaning of the word is shell-fish. Opponenauhock, now Apponaug. It was a great place of resort to the Indians, as appears by banks of clam-shell dust left by them.

Aquabapaug, POND, near the head of Pawcatuck river, near and below Chipchug. S. W. from S. Kingstown depot, one mile. Probably Worden's Pond. The name means muddy water.

Anaquatucket, RIVER. Orkatucket. S. and S. West of Wickford, and within one mile of it. The road to Boston Neck and Tower Hill crosses it a mile S. from Wickford.

Aquopimokuk, ISLAND, now GOULD'S Island, off Newport, once owned by Sachem Koskotop, who sold it to Gould. It is the most northern isle off Newport Bay, being nearly a mile N. W. from the Alms-house at Coaster's Harbor.

Aquidnesuk, ISLAND, now Small or Dutch Island, near Potter's factory, at S. Kingstown ferry. It was occupied by the Dutch sent from N. Y. as a fur trading place, before the Pilgrims landed at Plymouth, or about 1616.

Assapumsik, BROOK, or spring, East from the great Elm in Johnston. Only a few rods distant N. E. is an Indian retreat, in a ledge of rocks.

Ascomacut, SAME as Misquamacut.

Aquitawoset, a TRACT of land purchased by Atherton, N. and N. E. of Wickford. Same as Aquidnesit or Quidnesit. It is the shore between Potowomut and Cocumscusset or Wickford.

Aguntaug, BROOK, near an island called Mincamekek, in Cedar-swamp near or in a great pond two miles due East from Westerly bridge, called Puscomattas pond, or Borden's pond. [Potter, page 65.*] Runs to the S. bend of Pawcatuck river, and thence to the North bend, at Ashawa.

Ashawa, or **wake** or **wague,** RIVER, runs to Potter's bridge and Ashawa village. It enters Pawcatuck river near its N. bend. From this junction the State line of Connecticut runs due N., and below, this river forms the State line to the ocean.

Ashagomiconset, LAND, through which Aguntaug brook runs before it enters the S. bend of Pawcatuck river. This Asha-gomiconset land and two ponds form a line that runs through the middle of Westerly.

Azoiquoneset or **Nonequasset,** ISLAND. Fox island, two miles S. E. from Wickford. It means *Spruce Pitch island.*

Akoaxet, RIVER, in Little Compton, about five miles S. E. from Seconnet.

Aspanansuck or **Hakewamepinke,** the residence of Wawaloam, wife of Miantinomy. Potter, page 248. Supposed to be at Exeter hill, on Ten Rod road.

Absalonomiscut, a TRACT of land on the west side of Johnston. The Seven Mile line ran parallel with Mooshassuck and Providence river, at Fox point. Johnston, west of this line, was called Absalonomiscut. See city records.

Ashunaiunk, RIVER, in Richmond, probably Beaver river. It rises north of Ten Rod road, enters the N. side of Richmond at Reynold's factory, passes parallel with the Usquebaug, E. side of Shannock hill, to near Clarke's mill.

Annawanscut, CREEK, in Barrington, near the brick-kilns, and leads from them into the bay, a little N. of Nayatt point.

Acokesit, RIVER. Judge Brayton thinks it is Acoaxet.

* History of Narraganset, a very valuable work, by Hon. E. R. Potter.

Awoshonks, swamp, S. end of Little Compton, a mile or two N. E. from Seconnet point. The Indian queen named Awoshonks resided near it.

Annaquacutt, pond, and farm of 446 acres; sold for the benefit of Col. Angell's regiment. R. I. schedules, June, 1791. In Tiverton.

Antaghantic, neck. Three miles west of Providence tide water shore, and about the west side of Neutaconcanut hill, near the river. [Land titles, Vol. 2, page 324.]

Absalona, hill. Two to three miles east of Chepachet.

B.

Bassoqutoquaug, a sachemdom; or **Basskutoquoge.** [Potter, page 63, and Land Evidence, Vol. 1st, page 33.] This was a sachemdom under Koskotop, who sold Aquopimekuk island to Gould.

Boxet, pond, near Tippecan pond, West Greenwich. Same as Wixerboxet.

Bapctaushat, tract. N. W. corner of Charlestown, adjoining Machaquamaganset. [See Potter's History, 249.]

C.

Chepachet, river and village, or **Chepatset.** Fifteen miles N. W. of Providence, on Branch river. It means Devil's Bag. A bag or wallet was found here, probably dropped by some hunter, and as no one could tell who, an Indian said it was the Devil. Hence Chepuck, *devil:* chack, *bag;* now converted into Chepachet.

Cowesit, lands, or **kesit** or **suck.** The *shore* between Apponaug and Greenwich village, including farms from the bay westward to Crompton mills and beyond. Sold to R. I. government, 1639, by Tacommauan and his son Wasewkil, and grandson Namowish.

Conob, pond, a few rods east of Brand's Iron Works, west side of Richmond.

Chisawannock, island, or **Chesawane.** Hog or Perry island. Mouth of Bristol harbor, and west of Bristol Ferry about half a mile. Owned by the children of the late Capt. Raymond Perry. There was a contest, for the ownership of this island, between Plymouth and Rhode Island.

Chemanguz, pond, or **Chemunganoc.** Same as Watchaug. Poquient brook runs from it in a N. W. direction. It is in nearly the centre of Charlestown.

Copassanatuxet, LAND. **Cepasnetuxet,** or **Occu-passuatuxet.** Henry Green farm. It lies on the north side of Gov. Francis's farm, and is of the same breadth, extending from the bay westward. It is the northern boundary line of Warwick.

Chipchug, POND, Duck pond. Probably either Sherman's or Teft's pond, in South Kingstown.

Chepinoxet, ISLAND, off *Cowesit* shore, near Baker's station and the summer residence of John Whipple. It means Devil's Island.

Cocumscusset, BROOK, or Cawcawmsqussick, is now called Stoney Brook. It is the south boundary of Quidnesit, and a little north of Wickford. It gives name to the harbor of Wickford, and to the land where the Updike and Congdon house stands. The first English house erected in Narraganset, was here, by Richard Smith, who kept an Indian trading house; as did also Roger Williams, many of whose letters date here. It was here that the Massachusetts troops marched from, and back to, in the Swamp battle. It was the mart of Indian trade of Narraganset shores two hundred years ago.

Chippuxet, RIVER, or **Chepachuack,** or **Chepacche-wag,** called also *Wawoskepog.* [See Potter, page 225,] deed of Nicholas Gardiner Jr., to John Thomas, state records. This river runs near S. Kingstown Depot, between it and the hill or village of S. Kingstown.

Chopmist, HILL, north-west corner of Scituate, running three to four miles N. and S.

Chopcquonset, FARM or POINT, a mile S. of Pawtuxet, owned by the heirs of the late Nicholas Brown, Esq.

Connimicut, POINT, Warwick, opposite Nayatt. (See Stephen's map); also a map by Des Barres, 1776.

Chibacoweda, ISLAND, **Chibachuweset** or **Chippa-curset,** Prudence Island in the bay, below Warwick neck point. It was presented by sachem Canonicut, to Roger Williams; or rather sold to Williams and Gov. John Winthrop, for twenty fathom wampum and two coats.

Cocumpaug, POND, or **Cockampoag,** on old map, two miles north from General Staunton's in Charlestown, about one mile long. In 1794, it was proposed in the legislature to divert the Paw-catuck river into the sea, by opening a channel from Champlin's bridge in a South East direction, to Cocumpaug pond, two and a half miles, and through this to Fort neck, by Meadow Brook, and there at Fort neck enter Pauwanganset pond, at the N. E. corner of Champlin's farm, near the highway, one and a half miles E. of Gen. Staunton's. The pond is in the centre of Charlestown, and one mile N. E. from Wotchaugh pond.

Chanangongum, LAND, in Nipmuck. [See Trumbul's History, p. 346, vol. 1.]

Crookfall, RIVER, a short distance west of Judge Man's house in Smithfield. Vol. 4., page 122 of town records of Providence. See Wasquodomesit. This is probably an English word; for *f* rarely, if ever, occurs in Indian words.

Conockonoquit, ISLAND, is *Rose Island,* off Newport, about one mile S. W. from the almshouse. Sold by Canonicus (formerly called Maussup.) to Peleg Sanford. 1675.

Chockalaug, RIVER, rises in the south side of Douglas, and runs towards the centre of Burrillville, at Wood's mill and Harris factory.

Canonicut, or **Quononaquot,** ISLAND, between S. Kingstown Ferry and Newport. It is Jamestown.

Cancumsquisset, TRACT. North Kingstown, between Wickford and Exeter. It makes the west side of N. Kingstown, and adjoins Cocumscusset, or Wickford.

Connaug, POND, **Westconnaug.** See Stevens's map. S. E. corner of Foster. Westconnaug purchase was south part of Foster. Scituate and Cranston; which lies to the S. West of the North branch of the Pawtuxet river. See plat of it in H. L. Bowen's office.

Cajacet, POINT, or shore on *Canonicut island,* near the north end and facing Portsmouth. [See Benedict Arnold's will.]

Chemunganock, HILL, in Charlestown, probably near Chemunganset Pond; which is the same as Watchaug Pond. It is in the centre of Charlestown.

Cajoot, MINE, of Blacklead, or Carburet of iron, at the foot of Tower Hill in S. Kingstown.

Chippecurset, ISLAND, *Prudence* same as Chipacoweda.

Cokesit, TRACT, in Little Compton, near Dartmouth. It seems there were two Indian places of worship in the town in 1700; one in Seconnet, and the other northward and eastward at Cokesit.

Conconchewachet LAND.

Cappacommock SWAMP, three or four miles north from the Pequod shore. Itsig nifies hiding-place, to which the squaws and children retired on the approach of boats. Another like it is *Owlshead,* called Ohomowauke swamp.

Canonchet, MILL SITE, S. W. of Fenner's hill one mile. The name was lately given in honor of Canonchet.

Chipachuack, or **ague,** LAND, is the S. E. corner of Hall's purchase of two miles, near and including S. Kingstown depot.

Chackapaucasset, or **Chackapacauset,** now called Rumstick point or neck, S. of Warren, in Barrington, [Gen. Fessenden.] Rumstick was applied to a portion of it as early as 1697, by whom and wherefore is not known.

Chachacust, NECK, meadow in Barrington. It is near Warren. [Gen. Fessenden.]

Canopaug, BROOK and SWAMP, in Scituate, on the east side, sometimes spelled in deeds Quonopaug. The brook rises from the swamp and runs westerly to Moshwansicut river.

Consamassett, TRACT, a part of Moshantatuck or Pawtuxet river.

E.

Easterig, HILL, or **Eascoheague,** S. West part of West Greenwich. The post-office there is so named. The signification of the word is, 'origin of three rivers.' It is a great place for shooting game.

Eackhonk, RIVER, in the edge of Connecticut, and runs into the Ashwague river.

Espowet, CREEK, or **Sapowet,** makes in from the river. It is near Dr. West's house and the bay, in the S. W. part of Tiverton.

H.

Homoganset, HUNTING GROUND, **Nonequasset,** or **quksett,** or **Kesikamuck.** The neck of land between Wickford and Anaquatucket river.

Hassanamesit, TRACT in Grafton, one of the principal towns of the Nipmuck Indians, whose south line extended probably into Rhode Island.

K.

Kickamuit, RIVER, means a back river. It is in the north part of Warren. It was also applied ,says Judge Brayton, to Apponaug mill stream, entering the N. W. corner of Greenwich bay.

Kickamuit, SPRING, at the extreme N. E. part of Bristol, a few rods from the Warren line. In Narraganset dialect, springs were called Watchkecum; clear spring, Mishamuit. On the other side of the bay springs were called Dashmuit, Ashimuit; but Kickamuit means clear spring.

Kittackamucket, or **Muckqui,** COVE, on R. Island.

Kesikomuck, same as Nonequasset or quksett or Homogansett, the neck between Wickford and Anaquatucket river.

L.

Louisquissett, RIVER, or **Loqusqusset,** TRACT of land' through which the turnpike runs at the Lime quarries, in Smithfield' on which Jenks lives and the late Elisha Olney.

M.

Manisses, Block Island, or **Monasses,** It means Island of little God.

Misquamacut, or **coke Manquock,** or **Astomacut,** means *salmon*. It is the neck of land on the east side of Pawcatuck river. [See Potter, page 242.] The town of Westerly went by this name until it was incorporated in 1669. This tract extends to Wecapaug brook, or boundary line between Westerly and Charlestown. Steven's map erroneously represents Misquamacut to run far eastward of Wecapeug brook. [See affidavits of Indians, in Potter, 248.]

Moshassuck, RIVER, or **Moosshausic,** means *moose hunting grounds*, and passes by Gen. Barnes's and along south of Horton's Grove, and receives West river at or near Philip Allen's print works, and near Corliss & Nightingales' factory. It is also applied to a river S. W. of Pawtuxet, near where Samuel Gorton lived, and where he wrote a letter, signed by all his company to Massachusetts government.

Mashapaug, POND, two miles S. W. from Providence bridge. There is also a Mashapaug pond in Old Warwick, sometimes called Pomamganset.

Mashapaug, BROOK runs S. from the pond.

Manipsconasset, ROCK, near Pawtuxet bridge.

Musquetuxet, TRACT, probably N. of Pawtuxet bridge.

Musquetohauke, or **haug,** a BROOK, two or three miles north west of Smithville Seminary, and crosses Conn. and R. I. Turnpike near Scituate Bank, and along the W. side of N. Scituate village, to Aborn & Allen's factory.

Moshwausicutt, POND, near and north of Smithville Seminary, and within sight of it. The river leading from it through Scituate village has the same name.

Masquachug, BROOK, Muddy brook, or **Maskachaug**, or **Mascachusett**, on old map. It is applied also to a *hill*, half way between Greenwich and Potowomut. Potter says at the mouth of Hunt's river.

Mascakonage, BROOK, or RIVER, and is applied to a tract of land called Wyaxcumscut, being a tract bought by Richard Smith, Gov. Winthrop and Major Allerton. It lies N. W. of Wickford, was bought from Coquinaquon sachem and son of Miantonomia.

Metacurset, TRACT, contiguous to the last or Mascakonage ; deeded by said sachem.

Muschaug, applied to two PONDS, N. E. by east, near Westerly, and near the ocean, sometimes called East and West Muschaug or Massachaug. The one farthest east is called Musquatang, and is also called Babcock's pond.

Muyquatage, or **aug**, LAND, between Ward's pond and Quonaquontaug pond, and Weecapaug brook, which here runs into Quonaquontaug pond at its west end, and was claimed as the eastern boundary of,—in or adjoining Charlestown.

Mattapoysett, RIVER, means *crying chief*, — in Swanzy. Gardner's neck, so called, is bounded by it.

Mattoonuc, NECK, and RIVER or BROOK, N. W. part of Point Judith, the river runs into Point Judith pond ; it crosses the road east of Judge Peckham's a little west of Wakefield. The name was given by M. C. Perry to his country place on the Hudson. Near this brook is the birth-place of the two Com. Perrys.

Miskianza, BROOK, called also **Shickasheen**. Its waters come from Yarcoo, through Barber's pond. The Stonington Railroad crosses it a few rods south of the road. Nearly opposite to this was the great Indian swamp fight, on the north side of the Railroad.

Mishnic, POND, West Greenwich, two or three miles south or south-west of Washington village.

Matomy, HILL, runs S. E. by East some miles and the turnpike crosses it near its south end, three miles S. E. of Chepachet.

Metacom, seat of King Philip, N. E. side of Mount Hope bay, at its base, and on land of the late Hon. James De Wolf.

Moshanticut, BROOK, or **Mashatatuck**, running near Knightsvile and west of Gorton Arnold's and falls into the Pawtuxet. It was sometimes called Shantituck.

Mettaubscut, an Indian village, once stood west from Cowesett shore, between Apponaug and East Greenwich. [See letter of Roger Williams.]

Mammaquaug, BROOK, running south from Hopkinton to the Pawcatuck river in N. W. corner of the town of Westerly. There is a small fish thus called.

Mashonaug, ISLAND, in Pauwanget pond, Charlestown, and near the east end of it. Three small islands, called Browning isles, are represented on an old map, in said pond.

Musquataug, POINT, or **Muxquataug,** just within the S. E. of Westerly.

Minnabaug, POND, of great length on the Charlestown beach. Marked in maps as Babcock's pond. [Potter, page 65.]

Minacommuck, ISLAND, in Westerly, near the west end of Cedar Swamp, and near a large pond called Pascommattos, marked as Borden or Chapman pond. It is about two miles due east from Westerly village. A brook leads from the Pascomattas pond to the most southerly bend of Pawcatuck river, called Aquantaug brook, and its course is through Ashagomiconset.

Muxqutah, a NECK OF LAND; same as **Weeapaug,** in Westerly.

Moonassachuet, RIVER. [Potter, 275.] It runs into the Pascachuto pond at the north end of Pettaquamscott river, from a northerly and north-westerly direction, through Silver Spring factory.

Moscotage, RIVER, same as Narrow or **Pettaquamscot.** It runs between Pettaquamscott rock and the bay N. and S. at the east side of Tower hill, from Pascachuto pond to the beach, running N. and S.

Manshuck, near the "Olney's Land." [See page 29, Vol. 1. Registry of Deeds of Providence.] It is near Olney's lane, N. E. of Constitution hill, Providence.

Mishowomet, Warwick neck, same as Shaomet.

Maskechusic, POINT, at the mouth of Hunt's river.

Molligwasset, TRACT, sometimes called **Wollimosset.** It is the same as Wannimosett,—Viall residence, in Barrington or Seekonk.

Metaluxet, RIVER, same as narrow or Pettaquamscott, S. Kingstown.

Mosskituash, CREEK, in Barrington. It means *grass* or *straw to lie on,* or *hay.* It is now called Viall's creek, the mouth of it being in Barrington.

3

Moscachuck, creek, north of Nayatt and running to the brick yard from the bay.

Montop, hill, changed by the English to Mount Hope, in Bristol. Near the residence of the late Hon. James D'Wolf.

Massatuxet, brook, between Westerly and Watch hill.

Massanegtocanch, tract, on the east side of Blackstone river, in the north part of Cumberland. [See deed of Wamsitta to Thomas Willet, in Bliss' History of Rehoboth, page 51,] where this is the name of the boundary sold to Willet.

Mamantapit, tract, or wading river or place, being another boundary of the same line of Willet's purchase last mentioned, and near the junction of Cumberland and Attleboro', in their northern line. [See deed in Bliss' History.]

Mattato, hill, in N. W. part of Providence county, probably in Burrillville. [See deed signed by Daniel Mathewson, 1719, vol. 4, page 28, Prov. Records.]

Mashaquamaganset, tract, N. W. corner of Charlestown to Pawcatuck river, including, probably, Poquyent brook, [See page 249, Potter,] and having Nisquitianxsett between it and the ocean, and Wecapaug on the west side and Seepooke on the east side.

N.

Nipmuck, country, from Blackstone river westwardly, to the Connecticut, including north part of Smithfield and Burrillville, and probably Douglas and Thompson, but the chief headquarters was at Oxford.

Nipmuck, hill, a ledge a few miles N.W. of Washington village.

Nassawket, shore, from Apponaug to Warwick neck, Green's point and Buttonwoods occupy a part of it.

Natick, falls and village, or **Natchick,** hill, S. W. of Providence, 8 miles.

Nonequit or **Namquit,** pond, near Tiverton Four Corners.

Neutaconcanut, mountain, two or three miles S. W. from Providence. A river or brook near its base has the same name, near which is Antaghantic neck.

Namcook, neck, or **Namacoke** or **Noomuck.** It signifies *bank* in Indian. The English name is Boston neck. It extends from Anaquatucket south to Potter's factory, in North and South Kingstown.

Nonequacket, or **quasset,** shore, same as Homoganset.

The shore between Sowanoxet, or Fox Island, and Wickford and Anaquatucket river.

Nantusinunk, ISLAND, called also **Nomsusmuck.** It is Goat Island in Newport Harbor, less than a quarter of a mile from the end of Long wharf.

Nonquit, or **quamquit,** COVE or NECK, south of Stone bridge, in Tiverton, and half-way to Seaconnet, and adjacent to the late Judge Durfee's residence, one mile south of four corners.

Nowesit, NECK, formed by Kickamuit, on the west side, and Montop or Mount Hope, on the east.

Nonquit, POINT, or **Namquit,** Gaspee point, or near it. [Judge Staples, page 229.]

Nippsatchuck, HILL, or **Sachuck,** N. E. two miles from Greenville, in Smithfield, probably Wolf's hill.

Nipsachet, SWAMP, joins the S. E. corner of Burrillville.

Namyak, TRACT, or **Namyake,** on the west side of Pawcatuck. It was the country of the Pequots. Cassasiminum, or mon, was appointed Governor by the Commissioners, 1655.

Nowpaug, TRACT, joined the latter. [See page 64.] Cashawasset was, at the same time, appointed Governor of the Pequots, at Pawcatuck and Wecapaug.

Neshungansct, BROOK. [See Potter, page 65.] Near the junction of Ashawake with Pawcatuck river.

Nianticut, or **Neanticot,** or **Nyantic,** COUNTRY of Ninigret, bounded by Wecapaug brook on the west.

Neekequawsce, POND, probably Quonaquontaug, in Charlestown; also called Narragansett pond.

Nashanticut, TRACT, Cranston, about the present place of the Friends' Meeting house.

Nisquitianxet, TRACT, east side of Misquamicut, and extending into Charlestown; bounded southerly by the sea, westerly by Wecapaug and Misquamacut, easterly by land bought by Smith and called Seepooke, and northerly by Machaquamaganset and Bapetaushat, a tract sold to William Vaughan, of Newport.

Nayatt, POINT, in Barrington, eight miles south of Providence; has a lighthouse.

Nautiganset, BAY, at the termination of Pawcatuck river, and bounded on the S. W. side by Tower Hill. It is the same as

Narraganset, BAY. "The name is derived from an island

west of Wakefield, between Pettaquamscot and Misquamacook. " The original meaning of the word unknown," says Williams.

Nis-wos-akit, TRACT, near Greenville, in Smithfield. [See page 163, Potter. Roger Williams's letter.]

Nanquacket, POND or COVE, within a mile of the Stone bridge, Tiverton. Sold for Israel angell's soldiers, for revolutionary services.

O.

Ohomawauke, SWAMP, or **Cappacommuck,** place of concealment, near Owlshead.

Occupasspatucket, COVE or UXET, near Gov Francis's, Warwick. It is printed in Walling's map, " Occu Pas Pawtuxet Cove."

Ouchamanunkanet, MEADOW. S. W. from Pawtuxet, and near it.

P.

Pawconakik, TRACT, or **Pacanoket,** embraced Bristol, Warren and Barrington, with part of Swanzey and Seekonk. It was also called Sowams, by the Narragansets; but Pawcanokik, by the Wampanoags.

Pettaquamscot, RIVER, or **Metatoxet,** NARROW RIVER, in South Kingtown, and runs parallel with the bay, from Pascachute pond to Whale rock, and is but a few rods East of McSparren and Tower hill.

Pettaquamscot, TRACT, or PURCHASE; a strip of land, running east from the Pier, in South Kingstown, due west to Charlestown, and along the south side of Worden's pond.

Pettaquamscot, ROCK, near the river of that name. It is on the west side of Narrow river, half a mile north east from Tower hill church, and half way, in a straight line to Narrow river, in South Kingstown.

Ponaganset, POND, near Pine hill, in Glocester.

Ponaganset, RIVER, leading from the same, and uniting with the Moswansicut, to form the north branch of the Pawtuxet.

Pawtucket, FALLS, four miles north of Providence, in North Providence. It means union of two rivers, and a fall into tide water, because there the fresh water falls into salt. [Potter, p. 266. Pequot Testimonies.]

Pawtuxet, FALLS, in the village of that name, four miles south of Providence.

Pocasset, RIVER, over which is thrown the Stone bridge. It is also applied to the country adjoining, eastward, called Tiverton. [See another Pocasset, or Ohasset, page 39.]

Pawtuxent, FALLS, near Westerly, in the Pawcatuck river.

Pomham, SHORE, in Seekonk, opposite Field's point and Pawtuxet. " Warwick Neck," says Judge Brayton, "belonged to Sachem Pomham. A controversy existed between Massachusetts and Rhode Island about the title to it, in which Benedict Arnold took part, and S. Gorton."

Pascoag, or **Pascoage**, RIVER and FALLS, south side of Burrillville. [See Registry of Deeds, Providence, page 160.]

Papasqaush, PENINSULA, Bristol, R. I. It is so spelled in the original Indian deed, and not Pappoose Squaw, as is generally supposed.

Poquiunk, BROOK, or **Poquinunk**, or **Poquiant**, in Charlestown, and runs from Chemunganse pond to Great, or Pawtuxet river

Pohoganse, POND, or **Mushuagusset**, or **Mushuaganic**, is now Bailey pond, in South Kingstown.

Pisquasent, LAND, in Charlestown. [Potter.]

Potowomut, or **Pootowoomet**, NECK OF LAND, where the Ives live. South west from Warwick Neck light-house two miles.

Pojack, SHORE, south of the mouth of Hunt's river, a little below and S. E. of Greenwich.

Pausacaco, POND, or **Ponscachuto**, at north end of Pettaquamscot or Narrow river. It is half way between the Willet farm and Stuart's birth-place, in S. Kingstown.

Pasquesit, ROAD, **Paskuisset**, running S. E. from Champlin's bridge, on the Pawcatuck river, at Mallerd's bridge, passing under it on the east side of the great Indian swamp, N. E. corner of Charlestown. A brook and pond of the same name, which enter Pawcatuck at Kenyon's mills.

Pawcatuck, BAY and RIVER, Westerly, the river rises partly in Connecticut, and makes a part of the boundary between it and Rhode Island.

Pawawget, POND, or **Powaget**, in Charlestown, sometimes called **Ninigret**. Half a mile east of Gen. Stanton's. An arm of this pond stretches north nearly to the highway, where is the Indian fort. It is very near the beach and begins S. W. from Champlin's farm.

Paquinapaquoge, MEADOWS, near Cocumscussit, or north-west of Wickford.

Pawamack, POND, same as Beach pond, north-west corner of Exeter.

Pocasset, RIVER, or **Pochasset**, rises in Johnston, passes Simmons' two factories and Sprague's print works, and enters the Pawtuxet at Whitman's rubber works, two miles from Pawtuxet village. It is also applied to Tiverton shore, as far south as the stone bridge. The Toskeyonke Indians lived on the bank of this river.

Poquiunk, BROOK, or **Potquient**, runs from Chemagase, or Watchoag pond into Pawcatuck river, at the N. W. corner of Charlestown. Its course is N. W. from Watchaug pond to the river.

Pondock, RIVER, runs partly in Rhode Island and into Conn. near Moosup factory.

Postatugock, LOT. [See Registry of Deeds, Prov. page 48, vol. 1.] It is on the Pawtuxet river, and was sold by Wm. Field to Wm. Carpenter.

Poscammattas, POND, near the west end of Cedar swamp, in Westerly, probably Borden or Chapman pond. The line described in Potter, [page 65] began at the east end of Long pond, and ran N. W. crossing the shore road to a small pond and swamp, thence north to Borden's or Chapman's pond, and through this to an island called Minnacommuck, and through Aguntaug brook, and thence by said brook to the south bend of Pawcatuck.

Passatuthousee, RIVER, about Devil's Foot, a little north by west from Wickford.

Paspatonage, BROOK, same as **Weecapaug**, near the line between Westerly and Charlestown.

Paquantuck, or **Poquanatuck**, STREAM, flowing from Poneganset pond, in Glocester, two miles east of Connecticut line, and south of a middle east and west line.

Pataconconkset, BOTTOMS. The Warwick north boundary line courses through Pataconconkset bottoms.

Pequot, RIVER, is Thames river, Connecticut.

Pequot, PATH, led along the bay through Wickford to Wakefield, and through Charlestown to New York. It is the old county road from Providence, along shore to New London and New York.

There are houses along this Pequot road wearing a very antique appearance.

Poppaquinnapaug, POND, now Fenner's pond, one mile and a half N. W. from Pawtuxet bridge, in a straight line.

Passconuquis, COVE, one mile and a third south of Pawtuxet. On the left of the entrance into it, is Gaspee point, where the Gaspee was taken. It is probably the same as Occupass, Pawtuxet river.

Posneganset, POND, or **Punhauganset,** or **Pushaneganset,** one mile and quarter S. W. of Pawtuxet.

Puncoteast, TRACT or NECK, the S. W. point of what is now called Tiverton. It is the neck between the east side of the bay and Nonquit pond, on the east. It was the field of several slight skirmishes between the Indians under Philip, and the soldiers under Church.

Paussachuco, POND, at the north end of Narrow river, and a little north of the boundary line between North and South Kingstown ; same as Passaiaco.

Poppanomscut, LANDS, the south of Barrington, generally including Nayatt. [Gen. Fessenden.] Same as Phebe's neck.

Puckhunk or **nuck,** HILL, N. Stonington, near Hopkinton, R. I. It is also called Pendleton's hill.

Pasipuchammuck or **Paschuchammuck,** COVE. It is an old mill cove in Warwick. says Judge Brayton. It runs from the shore between Nassauket and Warwick neck, in a N. W. direction. [See Stevens' map.]

Pachet, BROOK, crosses the town line between Little Compton and Tiverton, soon joins the stream coming down from Nonquit point, and discharges into the bay, half-way between Stone bridge and Seaconnet point.

Pesquamscot, POND, called, also, Warden's, making nearly the N. E. boundary of the Indian lands, which begin at Cross' Mill, and follow the brook up to a little west of the pond, and then strike a brook that runs into Paweatuck river, at Zachery's bridge, and follows this to Shaddock's weir bridge, and thence south by Weecapaug, to the great East and West road, and follows this to Christopher Champlin's farm.

Peteconset or **quonset,** BOTTOMS, on the border marshes of Pawtuxet river, near the village of Pontiac Mills, or Clarkeville.

Q.

Quidnesit, or **Aquidesit,** or **Opuitowaxet,** from Pootowoomet to Cocumscusset or Wickford, along the shore.

Quawquinnippau, POND, south of Pawtuxet, called also Long pond.

Quidnic, RIVER, one of the western branches of the Pawtuxet river, through Washington village. Its reservoir is near Harkney mills in Coventry, and Quidnic pond. It is near Week's hill.

Quatuck, RIVER, or **Quequatasia,** or **Quequatage,** two miles up Pawcatuck river, near where Crandall's mill stood in 1681, [Potter,] on the north side, and near the centre of Charlestown.

Quoaug, ROCK, on the shore N. E. of Point Judith.

Quonnoquon, RIVER, enters the north side of Tiverton.

Quequechan, SHORE, from Fall River to Taunton.

Quonset, POINT, makes the right border of the entrance into Wickford bay, being the most projecting point.

Quequatage, and **Quequathanock,** same as Quatuck.

Quinsnaket, LEDGE OF ROCKS, S. W. and near the residence of the late Stephen Smith, Esq., and extending west to the Louisquisset turnpike, near Esquire Olney's. The name means *rock-house,* and is applied to places under shelving rocks. Another place of like form and name is near Woonsocket.

Quononoquot, same as **Canonicot.**

Quinamogue, MEADOW, in Westerly purchase. [See Potter, 204.] N. W. corner of Westerly, near Weir bridge.

Quequataug, UPLAND, running into the Great Indian Cedar Swamp, in Charlestown. [Potter.]

Quacut, NECK, abbreviation of Nonniquatuc, near Howland's ferry, in Tiverton.

Quassakonkanuck, POND, N. W. from the snuff mill at the head of Narrow river, South Kingstown.

Quonaquonset, MEADOWS, in Little Compton.

Quotenis, ISLAND, in Narraganset bay, was made an Indian fur trading place by the Dutch West India Company, settled in New York, 1617 or 18 and is now called Dutch island. [See page 268 Broadhead's history.]

Quamatucumpic, LAND, near Yawgoo, (or loo,) pond, and Barber's pond, within from one to two miles from North Kingstown depot. It makes the N. E. corner of Hall's purchase, so called, of two miles square; whilst Chippachuac makes the S. E. corner of said two miles purchase, to the brook south of South Kingstown depot. Quowachauk, or Whatchaug, makes the S. W. the corner of Hall's purchase, or "Usquepaug river on the west, Pettiquamscot purchase, on the east."*

Quinamogue, MEADOW, in Westerly purchase. It is near the N. W. corner of Charlestown.

Quawawchunk, about the swamp fighting ground, two or three miles west of South Kingstown depot.

S.

Saconnet, POINT, or **Seaconnet.** South west termination of Little Compton. In 1700, there were 100 Indian men here, and a smaller settlement north east, near Dartmouth. The boundary of the Saconnet Indians, on the north side, was a line from Packet brook to the head of Coaxet. The word, Seconnet, means black goose, like Seekonk. [See introductuory remarks.]

Scatacook, LANDS, or **Scatacosh,** part of Kent county.

Seekonk, RIVER and TOWN, opposite Providence, in Massachusetts. Name derived from Seki, black, and konk, goose. It has recently been decided to annex this town to Rhode Island. It is believed from tradition, that wild geese, in migrating, stop here to feed.

Shawomut, NECK. Warwick Neck. The Indian word means a spring. Boston was so called, from a spring. Also, a tongue of land, running from Slade's ferry, south west, near Tiverton.

Sowams, LAND, or **Sowamset,** part of Barrington and all of Warren and Bristol.

Sowamset, RIVER, now Warren river; also the name of the present site of Warren village, and of a bank there.

Sachueeset, POINT and BAY, making the S. E. point of Rhode Island, mentioned in Church's History of the Indian Wars. It is nearly opposite and N. W. from Seaconnet point.

Shannock, HILL, or **Mishannoke,** HILL, S. E. corner of Richmond. The name means *squirrel.*

Swamcot, NECK, on the east side of Pawcatuck river; same as Misquamacut.

*Hall's purchase. By this be it understood, that John Warner bought of a sachem, two miles square, and then deeded it to Henry Hall; and hence called Hall's purchase. East side of it being the west side of Pettaquamscot, or Narrow river, and called Quanatumpic,

4

Sowanoxet, ISLAND. Fox Island, near Wickford.

Shickasheen, same as **Miskianza,** BROOK. It runs from Yagoo and Barber's pond, in South Kingstown.

Saccanosset, HILL, a coal mine, in Cranston, near Gorton Arnold's, three and half miles west by south from Pawtuxet.

Shumunkanuck, HILL, N. W. corner of Charlestown, near the Stonington Railroad, and south side of it, midway between Watchaug pond and Richmond Switch, which bears due north one and a half miles.

Shamcook, BANK or SHORE, same as Namcook or Naomuck, Boston neck, in North Kingstown.

Spoart, LAND, between Nomquit pond and Nonequacket neck, Tiverton.

Swamicott, VALLEY, two miles S. E. of Chepachet. East of it is Matomy hill, running north and south.

Sachues, RIVER, near the old dividing line between Newport and Portsmouth, half a mile south of the latter. [Bartlett's Revised Statutes, p. 109.]

Seconiquouset, see **Quonset.**

Showatucquese, STREAM, or **Shewatuck,** very small, near Wickford or Cocumscusset bay. [See Potter's History, page 33. Land Records, page 57.]

Sawgoge, or **—goog,** POINT, in North Kingstown, extension of Sawgogue Meadows.

Sawgogue, MEADOWS, near Cocumscussit, mentioned in Coquinoquand's lease to R. Smith. [See Potter, page 33.] It is between Wickford and Devil's Foot.

Squamicott, WESTERLY, same as Misquamicutt.

Saweatucket, RIVER, South Kingstown, runs from Moore's-field, nearly due south, through Peacedale to Wakefield.

Shewtuck, RIVER or CREEK, see **Showauckese.**

Seepoke, or **Sepooke,** TRACT of land R. Smith bought of the Indian, Hermon Garret, [Potter's History,] adjoining the west side of Weecapaug line, where Charlestown and Westerly join, probably including the eastern part of the town of Charlestown, and the western part of South Kingstown.

Sheganiscalhoke, LANDS. It applies to the east side of the boundary between Westerly and Charlestown.

Sogkonate, POINT, same as Seeconnet.

Scamscammuck, SPRING, near Rumstick point, in Barrington. [Gen. Fessenden.]

Shannock, RIVER, in North Stonington, runs into Pawcatuck river, N. W. corner of Westerly. It means *squirrel river.*

Shippaquonset, LAND, near Passanoke, or quke, in South Kingstown. [See Potter.]

Suckatunkanuck, HILL, a mile or two west of Newtaconquenut hill, in Johnston, and ranging nearly parallel with it.

Sneechteconnct, RIVER, is the Blackstone river, running through Woonsocket and Mannville.

Shantituck, BROOK, Cranston, called also Meshantituck. A Quaker Meeting house was not far from here. [See Staples, p. 430.]

Sautaug, POND, north end of Long Island.

Seewamuck, POINT, nearly three miles northwest of Slade's Ferry, a point of land where Taunton river enters Montop bay. [De Barre's map.]

Sapowet, SHORE, or **Espowet**, between Dr. West's house and the bay in southwest part of Tiverton.

Suker, POND, runs into Chepachet river, one mile northeast of the village, from a north direction.

Sneech, POND, in Cumberland, a mile N. E. of Cumberland hill.

Sassawitch, BEACH, next beyond the present one of bathing in Newport.

Senechataconet, TRACT, between Abbott's run and the Blackstone or Sneachteconnet river, and extending north to the Massachusett's boundary line. It is a part, if not all, of Cumberland gore. [See old map in Arnold's History, 2d vol.]

T.

Tippecanauril, POND, or **Tippecanset**, or **Tippecan**, S. W. corner of West Greenwich.

Tockwotten, TRACT, S. E. portion of Providence city.

Tuscatucket, RIVER, three miles E. N. E. of Apponaug.

Tunipus, POND, very small, in Little Compton. It means *little herring*, is near the S. E. corner of the town.

Tommaquaug, or **Tommoeweague**, BROOK, runs from Hopkinton South to Pawcatuck river, near the N. E. corner of Westerly.

Toweset, or **Towesit**, NECK, on the Swanzy line, N. E.

from Bristol three miles, and two miles N. by E. from Montop, and and E. side of Warren.

Tiscatuck, a small, round swamp, near the centre of Westerly.

Tishcottic, FARM, in Westerly, once owned by Samuel Ward. The name is still retained.

Tobyan, SWAMP, between Cockompaug pond and the county road, within one mile due north from the old Dutch or Indian fort, in Charlestown.

Teapannock, POND, near the sea shore, probably Babcock's pond in Westerly. It has another Indian name.

Tommany, HILL, an abbreviation of Wannametonomy or Wonnemetonomy, north of Newport.

Tuncowsden, POINT, India point, in Providence. [See map of 1741, inserted in history of boundary line in Massachusetts.

Tismattuc, LINE, same as Weacapaug or Weepacannock, between Westerly and Charlestown.

Tonissit, NECK, lower or south end of Warren—mostly in Warren.

Tauskounk, or **Toskiounke,** MEADOW, below Pontiac. There was an Indian tribe here. [See Vol. 5, page 9, of Providence Records.

Tittient, ROAD, leading out from Newport. [See Bartlett, Vol. 1, page 57.]

U.

Usquebaug, RIVER, or **Osquepaug,** or **Wawaskepaug,** west boundary of S. Kingstown, running from Exeter due South till it meets a stream coming from Warden's pond, and thence running to Shannock mills.

W.

Weecapaug, NECK and BROOK, or **Musqutah,** or **Paspataug,** or **Paspatonage,** or **Tismatuc,** or **Waxcadowa.** It runs southerly, and enters the west end of Quanaquataug pond. It was regarded as the boundary between the Pequot and Nyantics.

Woonsocket, HILL and FALLS. The hill is a mile or two south west from the compact part of the village or falls. It was formerly spelled Wonsocket. [Providence Records, vol. 4, p. 28.]

Wamkeag, HILL, or **Wayunkeak.** [Roger Williams.] Two miles north east of Greenville, and extending to Farnum's, or Slaterville turnpike,

Woonasquatucket, RIVER, divides North Providence from Johnston.

Wesquanage, or **aug**, SETTLEMENT. [Bartlett, page 440, vol. 1. See Arnold, vol. 1, page 5.]

Wannomoisset, TRACT. Viall region, head of Bullock's Cove, near which, on the Warren and Providence road, was the residence of Thomas Willett, who was buried on the east bank of the cove.

Wawweponseag, SHORE. Blackstone's residence, near Lonsdale. It means place for snaring water fowl.

Wolopeconcet, POND, or **Pawcomet.** Beach pond, on Lockwood's map.

Wanwaskepaug, same as Usquepaug. It is the north west corner of Hall's two mile purchase, at Mumford's mills.

Wima-tom-pic, LAND. Part of Hall's purchase.

Weybosset, STREET, in Providence. It means half way.

Wanshuck, MEADOWS. in North Providence, probably where Wainscott factory is. [See deed, vol. 11, p. 36, City Records.]

Wampnesick, applies to Pawtucket. [See page 292. Potter. Deed to Fones.]

Wincheck, POND. The eastern one on the beach, in Charlestown, called on Stephen's map, Green hill pond.

Wolopeconnet, POND, **Poncamac**, or BEACH POND, probably Babcock's pond, Westerly.

Watesamoonsuck, TRACT and HILL, west of Hopkinton.

Wyaxumscut. See **Muscakonage.**

Wasquadomesit, or **Westquadomesit**, RIVER and LAND, between Limerock and Mansville. [Page 14, vols. 1 and 4, Providence Records.] It extends north to Judge Mann's. On Steven's map, called Crookfall. [See deed, vol 4, p. 177.]

Weepoiset, in Swanzey. [Church's Indian Wars, p. 87.]

Wyapumscat, LAND, or **Maskacowage**, or **Cocumscusset**, bounded by the brook on the west side.

Wincheck, POND, at Rockville village, near the northwest corner of Hopkinton.

Wickaboxet, POND, north of the southwest corner of West Greenwich.

Wesquogue, TRACT and POND, near Watson's Pier, a little north of it, and northeast from Tower Hill, and between Pettaquamscot and the bay.

Watuppa, NORTH, POND, in the southeast corner of Tiverton. It lies chiefly in Massachusetts, the south part being in Rhode Island.

Watuppa, SOUTH, POND, in the northeast corner of Tiverton, near North Watuppa. The road from Fall River to New Bedford crosses between the two Watuppas.

Wonnumetonomy, HILL, see Metonomy, north of Newport.

Wannuchecomecut, a part of Boston neck, in North Kingstown.

Wappewassick, ISLAND. Prudence. [See Bartlett's Records, vol. 1, page 31.]

Watchemottuck, or **moyket,** NECK, from India bridge to Bowers' cove, and near Kettle point. [See note in Bliss' History,] from which it appears to include all between Ten Mile river and Bullock's cove and Pawtucket river.

Witchetseconnet, LANDS, or **Wecatheconnet,** between Apponaug and Arnold's factory, and between Natick and Apponaug.

Watcheer, ROCK, where Roger Williams is supposed to have landed. This, however, is an expression in old English, equivalent to " How do you do ?"—and was used by Indians to welcome Roger Williams when he landed.

Wapanoos, POINT, is Point Judith. By the Dutch, the name was applied to all Narraganset. [See Broadhead's map in Dutch History of New York.] The Indian name before the Dutch arrived, was *We-nan-na-toke.* [See the word.]

Watchaug, POND, near the centre of Charlestown. It discharges into the Pawcatuck river, by Poquiunk brook, near Brown's bridge. Same as Chemunganock.

Woonachasset, or Coasters Harbor, off Newport. The site of the Asylum. It is a peninsular.

Weeweonk, CREEK, or **Wawweonke,** that makes in near Nassawket from Greenwich bay, not far from the Buttonwoods.

Wawattaquatuck, TRACT, or corner of the tract owned or claimed by Herman Garrett, in Charlestown,—northwest corner of it.

Wotesamoonsuck, POND, which sends a branch into Ashaway river in Hopkinton, and is on the Connecticut line.

Washukquatom, HILL. [See page 32, Vol. 1, Registry of Deeds, Providence.] It is in Burrillville.

Westototucket, RIVER, either Beaver or Usquepaug. [See Potter, page 66.] It is in S. Kingston.

Westquanoid, PURCHASE, or **Westconnaug,** being a strip of land, the south line of which runs through the State E. and W. from Connimicut point, opposite Nayatt on the bay, through the centre of Punhanganset or Great pond, through Natick to the Connecticut line. [See page 72, Vol. 4, Providence Records.]

Woxeodawa, same as **Weeapaug,** being the boundary between Pequots and Nianties.

Wickerboxet, POND, west side of West Greenwich, probably same as Boxet.

Wallum, POND, N. W. part of it in Burrillville.

Westconnaug, RESERVOIR, south of Clayville, in Foster.

Waypoyset, NARROWS, at the entrance of Kickamuit river, which runs north and south through the eastern part of Warren.

Woquagonset, POND, or LITTLE POND, in Old Warwick, south side of the road that runs from Pawtuxet to Apponaug. On Stevens's map it is called Sand point, or pond.

Wawashekit, LAND, north west of Pawtucket Falls.

Wequechackomuck, LAND, south of Natick, and near Emanuel Rice's farm.

Wethungamet, CREEK, or **Wawconk,** CREEK, east or north of Baker's station, Coweset shore

Weehenama, MEADOW, or **Nonganeek,** between Old Warwick and Pawtuxet river. West and south west from the bridge.

Watachun, SPRING, on the south side of Greenwich, near the mouth of Muscachowage river.

Wiorickheague, or **Winkheigues,** or **Wayunckeke,** SETTLEMENT. [Potter, p. 163.] North from Greenville, and including a hill. [Bartlett, vol. 4, p. 371.]

Wicketiquack, COVE, in Stonington, midway between Stonington and Westerly.

Winscot, RIVER, or **Wanshuck,** or **Manchuck,** where Wainscott factory is, in North Providence.

Wyapumseat, a RIVER, in the north part of Quidnesit. Same as Mascachowage.

Weekachommet, TRACT. Same as **Wequechacommuck.**

Washukquatum, HILL. [See vol. 1, of recorded deeds.]
It is in Burrillville.

Winnatompic. [See same volume.]

We-nan-na-toke, or **Weyanitoke,** POINT JUDITH, or
JUDA-NECK, deeded by Tumtockoro, Indian chief, 1659, to Winthrop
and others. [See Land Evidence, vol. 1, page 29.]

Y.

Yawgoog, POND, on the corner line and northwest corner of
Hopkinton.

Yawgunsk, BROOK, on the east side of Ninagret's fort. It is
probably the Cross' Mill brook, in Charlestown.

Yawcook, PONDS, about two and half miles northwest from
South Kingstown station, and on the line between Exeter and Richmond.

Yawgoo, WOODS, west from Gardner's Mill, and north of Yawgoo pond.

———

There are several places bearing the same name, in Massachusetts
and in Rhode Island :—

Mashpoag, POND, in Sharon, and Cranston, R. I.

Coweset, TRACT, in Wareham, and East Greenwich, R. I.

Winnemoiset, in Braintree, and Bullock's cove, R. I.

Secconnosset, in Plymouth, near Gorton Arnold's, R. I.

Pocasset, RIVER, Stonebridge, and a river near Spragueville,
R. I.

Pawtuxet, now Plymouth, and in Cranston, R. I.

www.ingramcontent.com/pod-product-compliance
Lightning Source LLC
Chambersburg PA
CBHW032144080426
42733CB00008B/1195